5 BEARS

ROB LAIDLAW

Fitzhenry & Whiteside

Published in Canada by Fitzhenry & Whiteside,
195 Allstate Parkway, Markham, ON   L3R 4T8

Published in the United States by Fitzhenry & Whiteside,
311 Washington Street, Brighton, MA 02135

Fitzhenry & Whiteside acknowledges with thanks the Canada Council for the Arts
and the Ontario Arts Council for their support of our publishing program. We acknowledge
the financial support of the Government of Canada through the Canada Book Fund (CBF)
for our publishing activities.

Library and Archives Canada Cataloguing in Publication
Title: 5 bears / Rob Laidlaw.
Other titles: Five bears
Names: Laidlaw, Rob, 1959- author.
Identifiers: Canadiana 20210093889 | ISBN 9781554554614 (hardcover)
Subjects: LCSH: Bears—Juvenile literature.
Classification: LCC QL737.C27 L35 2021 | DDC j599.78—dc23

Publisher Cataloging-in-Publication Data (U.S.)
Names: Laidlaw, Rob, 1959-, author.
Title: 5 Bears / Rob Laidlaw.
Description: Markham, Ontario : Fitzhenry & Whiteside, 2021.| Summary: "Stories of 5 bears
show what their lives were, and are, really like and the issues and challenges that all bears face.
Bears deserve our respect, compassion and protection. Today, bears in the wild are threatened
and many bears in captivity are suffering. They need our help to ensure they survive and
prosper in the years ahead" -- Provided by publisher.
Identifiers: ISBN 978-1-55455-461-4 (hardcover)
Subjects: LCSH Bears —Juvenile literature. | Captive wild animals – Juvenile literature. |
Animal welfare – Juvenile literature. | Human-animal relationships – Juvenile literature. |
BISAC: JUVENILE NONFICTION / Animals / Bears.
Classification: LCC QL737.C27L353 |DDC 599.78 – dc23

Edited by Kathy Stinson
Text and cover design by Tanya Montini
Additional images licenses from Shutterstock, iStock and Alamy
Printed in Hong Kong by Sheck Wah Tong Printing

www.fitzhenry.ca

CONTENTS

INTRODUCTION

It was late in the evening as I was driving north on the Icefields Parkway from Alberta's Banff National Park to Jasper National Park when I noticed a brown shape on a grassy area beside the highway. As I approached I saw it was a grizzly bear. Then, to my great surprise, I also saw two cubs. It was a mother and her babies. No one else was around. I was alone with the three bears. I sat in the car and watched them play and forage in the grass and nearby bushes. About 10 minutes later, they slowly ambled away and vanished into the trees.

Just 30 minutes later, I encountered two young black bears playing rough-and-tumble with each other as they moved along the edge of the forest before running down a steep embankment onto a gravel covered riverbank. I watched them through my binoculars. They seemed to be having fun as they travelled east along the river, until they finally disappeared over a faraway ridge.

Throughout the years, I've encountered a lot of bears. Sometimes they were wild, like the ones I've described above, but hundreds have been in captivity, confined in zoos and circuses. As a professional animal advocate I've done my best to help bears by conducting campaigns to end their neglect, abuse and suffering and to keep them in the wild, where they belong.

Our relationship with bears is complex. Some people think of bears as big, cuddly pets, while others see them as dangerous, wild animals. Many people want bears left undisturbed in the wild, while others want to hunt and kill them, confine them in zoos or use them for their fur, meat or body parts.

It's clear that bears are popular animals almost everywhere in the world. They're featured in fables, cartoons, children's books, television shows, documentary films and other media. In *5 Bears* I mention two that have become famous: Winnie, the real bear that led to the story *Winnie the Pooh*, and Wojtek, the soldier bear who became a war hero. I also talk about lesser known bears like Yupi,

a polar bear who lived in Mexico, Jasper, who was rescued from a bear farm in China, and Vince who now lives at a sanctuary in the United States. I hope their stories show what their lives were, and are, really like and the issues and challenges that all bears face.

There are many myths and misunderstandings about bears. In *5 Bears* I hope to set the record straight and convince you that bears deserve our respect, compassion and protection. Today, bears in the wild are threatened and many bears in captivity are suffering. They need our help to ensure they survive and prosper in the years ahead. I hope after reading this book you'll decide it's time for you to do your part to help bears.

Rob Laidlaw
Award-winning children's author
Executive Director, Zoocheck

THE BEAR FACTS

WHAT IS A BEAR?

Bears are mammals in the Family Ursidae. Today there are eight species of bears and they are found in habitats ranging from tropical rainforest to Arctic pack ice, and on every continent except Australia and Antarctica. They are well equipped to survive with relatively large, stout bodies, large legs, long snouts, short tails and non-retractable claws. Most bears are predominantly omnivorous, with the exception of the Giant panda which eats mostly bamboo and polar bears which are the most carnivorous bears. In some regions, such as the Pacific coast forests of Canada, bears are a keystone species that serve a vital role in the ecosystems they inhabit.

BEAR ANCESTORS

Bears probably evolved from a small carnivorous animal that existed 30 - 40 million years ago, but it wasn't until about 20 - 27 million years ago that the first true bears emerged. The common ancestor

Giant short faced bear skeleton

for modern bears is thought to be *Ursavus elemensis*, a long extinct animal about the size of a small dog. About 5 – 10 million years ago, the giant panda and *Ursus* bears appeared, including one called the Auvergne bear *Ursus minimus*. Other bear species followed including the Cave bear and the fearsome Giant Short-faced bear in North and South America. In time, most of those species disappeared. The most recent species of modern bear is the polar bear who evolved over the last 200,000 – 300,000 years from brown bears. In fact, the two species are so closely related they can interbreed. Their hybrid young are called pizzly bears or grolar bears.

MODERN BEARS

Giant panda (*Ailuropoda menlanoleuca*)

The Giant panda is one of the most popular animals in the world due to its unique black and white coloration. They are found in China's high-altitude bamboo forests and inhabit home ranges just a few square kilometers in size. They are the most vegetarian of bears and subsist mostly on bamboo. Giant pandas tend to be more active at night and spend most of their time on the ground, even though they are good climbers. Wild panda population estimates vary from about 1,600 to as many as 3,000, but their habitats are severely threatened by deforestation and development.

Asiatic Black Bear *(Ursus thibetanus)*

These medium-sized bears with a black or dark brown colour, light muzzle and a long-hair ruff around the neck are found in forested areas where they can often be seen high in the trees. They have a distinctive white, crescent-shaped, chest patch, so they are sometimes referred to as moon bears. Asiatic black bears are relatively nocturnal and subsist on a varied diet of plant and animal materials. They are found over a wide range of Asia, including Vietnam, Cambodia and Thailand, in mountainous regions of northern India, Nepal, Pakistan and Afghanistan, as well as parts of China, Taiwan, Japan and Russia.

Sloth Bear *(Melursus ursinus)*

Sloth bears are largely insectivorous and feed extensively on termites, but they will also eat other insects, honeycombs, bird's eggs, carrion and some vegetation. Their extremely long claws are adapted for tearing apart termite mounds and nests. Their front upper teeth are missing, so they have a gap through which they suck up termites. Their slurping can be heard from quite a distance. They are medium-sized bears with a long shaggy coat that are found from the dry grasslands and forests of northern India to the more humid tropical forests in southern India and Sri Lanka. In addition to being threatened by habitat destruction, sloth bears are also killed by poachers for their body parts, particularly their gallbladder. In the past, sloth bear cubs were also captured to be cruelly used as dancing bears on the streets.

Sun Bear *(Helarctos malayanus)*

Inhabiting the dense tropical forests of Southeast Asia, Sun bears are the smallest of bears. These largely nocturnal predators constantly forage for food, which can include insects, lizards, small mammals, eggs and vegetation. They are mobile on the ground but are also adept at climbing high into the trees to search for fruit or to construct nests made of branches where they spend their days. Their long claws aid in both digging and climbing. They have short, dense, dark fur with a blond or golden crescent on their chest, the marking that gave them the name Sun bear. Since they are nocturnal forest dwellers, not as much is known about Sun bears as other bear species, but it is thought that their numbers are diminishing due to destruction of their habitat and poaching for their body parts.

Spectacled Bear *(Tremarctos ornatus)*

Also known as the Andean bear, this small, shaggy-furred bear is black or dark brown in colour and usually has white or yellowish markings that extend from above the eyes down over the muzzle to the chest. It is South America's only native bear species and is found in relatively small, fragmented populations in the Andes mountains of Peru, Ecuador, Bolivia, Columbia and Venezuela. Exact numbers are not known but it is thought there could be about 20,000 individuals left in the wild. Spectacled bears are primarily vegetarian and eat a wide variety of plant materials, including tough palm nuts and cactus. However, like most bears, they will also consume insects, small animals and carrion when available. They live in a variety of habitats including dry forests, rainforest, and even coastal scrublands.

American Black Bear (*Ursus americanus*)

By far the most populous species, the American black bear is found throughout North America in a variety of primarily forested habitats. Depending on food availability their home ranges can vary from a dozen square kilometers to several thousand. Equipped with strong, curved claws, these medium-sized bears are good tree climbers, diggers and very capable swimmers. They prefer dense vegetation where there are large quantities of edible plant and animal material, including insects, bird's eggs and small mammals. Some black bears prey on deer fawns, moose calves and other animals. In areas with seasonal salmon runs, they may be good fishers as well. Estimates place the number of black bears in North America at anywhere between 600,000 and 900,000.

Brown Bear (*Ursus arctos*)

Their large size, distinctive shoulder hump and long claws make brown bears easy to recognize. The brown bear is now found in parts of North America, a few areas of Europe, northern Russia, Asia and northern Japan. Inland living brown bears in North America are called Grizzly bears because of white-tipped fur that give them

a grizzled appearance. Brown bears eat mostly plant material, but will also eat insects, eggs, birds, small and large mammals and fish. They'll catch salmon migrating up rivers and streams to lay their eggs, but they can also hunt larger prey such as elk, caribou and moose. There could be as many as 200,000 brown bears surviving in the wild with the largest number in Russia, followed by the United States (mostly in Alaska) and Canada.

Polar Bear *(Ursus maritimus)*
The polar bear is the largest land carnivore in the world. Polar bears feed mainly on seals, but also scavenge for carcasses of whales and walruses. They also consume reindeer, small mammals, birds, eggs, fish, vegetation and human refuse. They are capable of eating as much as 20% of their body weight at one time. Each polar bear has its own home range which varies in size, from a couple of thousand to tens or hundreds of thousands of square kilometers, depending on food availability and weather conditions. Individual home ranges may overlap with those of other bears. They are outstanding swimmers and superbly adapted to living in the cold. Their total number is estimated at approximately 25,000, with the largest number in Canada.

Sloth bears have the longest paws and claws (relative their size) of any bear. They use their almost 10 centimeter claws for digging up insects such as ants and termites.

2

BUILT LIKE A BEAR

WALKING ON PAWS AND CLAWS

Bears walk in a flat-footed fashion, called **plantigrade locomotion**. Just like people, when bears put their feet down, the heel contacts the ground first and the foot rolls forward with the toes (and claws) being the last part of the foot to leave the ground. The front legs are longer than the hind legs and are a bit pigeon-toed, so bears always seem to have an awkward gait. But they can move very fast when they want to, sometimes as fast as a racehorse.

Giant Short Faced Bear
Extinct

Cave Bear
Extinct

Polar Bear

All bears have five, non-retractable claws on each foot. The front claws are the longest and are great tools for digging, tearing, climbing, manipulating objects or self defense. The Giant panda has a sixth toe (an extension of the wrist bone that's similar to a thumb) that is used to help grasp the bamboo stalks they eat.

THE NOSE KNOWS

Smell is extremely important to bears. It is used to locate food, find mates and to identify and avoid danger. Based on the number of scent receptors, bears probably have the best sense of smell of all land animals, even better than tracking dogs like bloodhounds. Polar bears are thought to have the most sensitive noses of all the bears. Evidence suggests they can pick up scents from a seal or whale carcass that is 40 miles (64 km) away. They can also smell a seal under 3 ft (.9 m) of snow.

Pandas are the only bear that have a 6th toe on their front paws. This extra claw acts like our thumb and allows the panda more control when handling food.

2 m

1 m

Brown (Grizzly) Bear   American Black Bear   Asiatic Black Bear   Sloth Bear   Giant Panda   Sun Bear

A polar bear's paddle-like, webbed feet are adapted for swimming and walking on ice. Their claws are relatively short and provide traction, while the fur between their toes and tiny bumps called papillae on the soles of their feet prevent slipping.

LOVING THE OCEAN AND THE COLD

Although most bears are good swimmers, Polar bears are the bear world's best. Their body shape is more elongated than other bears, their heads are small compared to overall body size, and their necks are relatively long and slender which makes them streamlined for swimming. They also have small, rounded ears that are laid

flat when swimming underwater. Their large paws, sometimes more than 12 inches (30 cm) across, and a partial membrane between their toes make their feet great for paddling too.

The large paws also help spread out weight as polar bears move across ice and snow, just like snowshoes do. Each paw is equipped with one non-retractable claw on each of its five toes, useful for gaining traction on slippery surfaces and for grasping prey. The sole of each foot has a thick black pad covered with tiny bumps (called **papillae**). Hairs growing between the pads and the toes also help prevent slipping.

Oily, water-repellent fur covers the entire body, except for the footpads (and, of course, the nose). Their dense under-hair insulates the body and is covered by a thinner layer of stiff, clear, hollow guard hairs, which create the polar bear's white look. Underneath their white fur, Polar bears have black skin (possibly an adaptation for absorbing sunlight) and a layer of insulating blubber that can be 4 – 10 cm (1.5 inches to 4 inches) thick.

Polar bears are astonishingly well adapted to the cold weather. When they are active, they can overheat when it's only 32°F (0°C). No other bear, and few other animals, are as suited to the cold as polar bears.

Polar bears are often considered to be marine mammals because they live on sea ice and along ocean coasts and are adapted for swimming. They have been encountered long distances away from land or ice floes.

A black bear emerges from its den. While bears do sleep the winter away they can wake up if a threat such as wolves (or in this case scientists) disturb the den.

HIBERNATION: THE LONG SLEEP

Bears are not true hibernators, but some, especially in regions with cold winters, go into a state of dormancy where their body temperature and **metabolic rate** decreases. They can go three to six months without eating, drinking, urinating or defecating. Hibernation is triggered by the change in seasons and the decrease in food supplies as winter approaches. It is an adaptation that allows bears to survive. If they didn't hibernate, they might starve.

Leading up to hibernation, bears go through a period of increased appetite called **hyperphagia**. As their internal clock shifts, the bears eat more and pack on fat for their hibernation period. They can gain huge amounts of weight. They need it, because a large bear can lose a pound or two (1/2 – 1 kg)

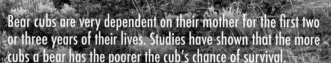

Bear cubs are very dependent on their mother for the first two or three years of their lives. Studies have shown that the more cubs a bear has the poorer the cub's chance of survival.

every day while hibernating. They can also wake up numerous times or even leave their dens on occasion.

Where bears don't experience seasonal food losses, they remain active all year round.

BEAR CUBS

Female bears typically give birth to young every two to four years, depending on their species. Two blind and helpless cubs (but sometimes 3-5) are born late in the year or in the spring. After 4 – 8 weeks the cub's eyes open and they are able to move around. They spend the next 16 – 24 months with their mother learning the skills necessary to survive before going off on their own. Mothers are very protective of their young and will lead them to safety if threatened. If necessary, they may also physically protect them, as they do when confronted by unfamiliar male bears who may want to kill their cubs.

Brown bear emerges from her winter den. While some bears do sleep the winter away, they can wake up several times, especially if they are disturbed.

Some call this the "polar dance". This is just a play fight between two bears of equal size. They are just having fun until the ice forms on Hudson's Bay and they can start to hunt seals again.

③

BEAR LIFE

DO BEARS HAVE FRIENDS?

Bears might spend a lot of time alone, but they are not entirely solitary. In fact, bears may form social hierarchies and have complex relationships with other bears. Males and females spend time together during mating periods, and females spend considerable time raising their cubs. Bears may also encounter each other periodically because their home ranges overlap or because they are attracted to an abundant source of food. Two examples are brown bears congregating at a favourite salmon stream during the migration of the fish upstream or Polar bears congregating in Churchill, Manitoba when they are waiting for Hudson Bay to freeze. Bears also share information by smelling the scent markings of other bears and/or leaving their own at rubbing spots and in deposits of urine and feces. Even when bears might seem to be alone, they may still know other bears are around.

Bears have excellent memories about where food can be found. Every year bears time their arrival to be at these falls when the salmon arrive. When food is abundant the bears share the space without many serious fights (a few will occur). Each bear knows its place in the hierarchy.

BEAR DAY

Bears are active animals, walking, climbing, swimming, foraging, hunting, investigating objects, like logs and rock piles, by touch, sight and smell, scent marking, scratching, digging, playing alone or with others, making day or night beds, and doing lots of other activities, many every day. Mothers watch over their cubs to make sure they are safe. Black bear females might signal their cubs to climb a tree if she perceives a threat, while sloth bear cubs may just climb up on their mother's back when they feel unsafe. Adult bears may travel in pairs or congregate at a good food source, like a favourite salmon stream or berry patch. Bears' days can vary according to their species, age, location, time of year and other factors.

In order to make the life of a captive animal more interesting zoos have resorted to presenting the animal's food in containers that either mimic the wild or challenge the animal's intelligence as in this case of a spectacle bear.

Garbage containers in bear country have changed throughout the years. Food scraps in old style bins are easy for bears to retrieve.

BEAR SMARTS

Bears have large, complex brains and can perform very complex tasks. Their excellent long-term memories help them remember and navigate through their home ranges, which can be hundreds or thousands of square kilometers in size. Bears can remember where they found food years before, when favourite food sites, such as seasonal berry patches, are best to visit, and times of danger, such as hunting seasons. They can solve problems too, like how to get into bear-proof garbage containers and bird feeders. Bears also have complex social interactions with other bears and that is usually a sign of smarts. Many experts believe bears are among the most intelligent of land animals.

BEAR TALK

Bears communicate with sounds that can include grunts, growls, huffs, snorts, moans, roars, whimpers and purring, to name just a few. When American black bears feel threatened, they will often huff,

Black bears clearly leave claw marks when they climb a beech tree because the bark is soft. Bear nests are a sign of a bear's feeding on the tree's mast (nuts, fruit or berries). An overturned rock is a sign that a bear has been looking for insects and grubs.

snort and grunt, while an angry brown bear may growl or roar. A contented spectacled bear may make a purring sound.

Body postures are also an important part of communicating what mood a bear is in. A lowering of the head might indicate submission, while an icy stare may be a sign of aggression.

Scent marking is also an extremely important form of bear communication. Rubbing their scent on trees or scenting trees, rocks or other features with urine or anal gland secretions leaves information for other bears to pick up. Hikers sometimes encounter signs of bear rubbing (and clawing) on trees that have been used by bears for generations.

LOOKING FOR A GOOD MEAL

Bears are largely **omnivorous** which means they eat both plant and animal foods. Since they are not very good at digesting plant material, bears eat a lot and prefer young, fresh plants that are easier to digest. The polar bear relies on the consumption of seals, walruses and other marine animals for survival. Most bears

A black bear's claw marks are very close to its foot prints; a grizzly's claw marks are well in front of its pad marks.

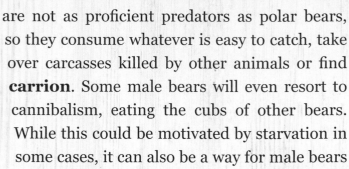

Bears can be scavengers or thieves. A brown bear scavenges a winter killed bison that has also been fed on by wolves, coyotes, ravens and grizzlies. A grizzly bear stands guard over a wolf-killed elk. The grizzly chased off the two wolves but in a short time the wolves returned and reclaimed their kill.

Plant eating animals tend to have big bellies and the Giant panda is no exception. To get nutrients out of plants takes a lot longer than to digest meat so animals that consume a lot of plant material tend to have large stomachs.

are not as proficient predators as polar bears, so they consume whatever is easy to catch, take over carcasses killed by other animals or find **carrion**. Some male bears will even resort to cannibalism, eating the cubs of other bears. While this could be motivated by starvation in some cases, it can also be a way for male bears to help ensure their **genes** are carried on. If unrelated cubs are killed, their mothers will be available for the males to breed with much sooner than if her cubs survive.

BAMBOO BEARS

The Giant panda spends a good portion of each day eating bamboo stocks, stems and leaves with their powerful jaws and large teeth. Remarkably, Giant pandas have also evolved flexible forepaws and a sixth toe to help them hold onto and manipulate bamboo stalks. Their carnivore digestive systems don't absorb much energy or protein from bamboo, so they have to eat 15 - 30 kg (33 - 66 lbs) per day. Pandas are not as active as other bears and their metabolism is lower, making it easier for them to subsist on poor food sources like bamboo.

After a lifetime behind bars in a small concrete pen, 34 year old senior brown bear Tanya was rescued by AMP and brought to the Libearty sanctuary in 2020.

BEAR SENIOR CITIZENS

In 2013, the world's oldest wild bear died of natural causes in the forests of northern Minnesota. She was 39 ½ years old. According to the Department of Natural Resources, the female black bear, known as Bear No. 56 (her study number) produced 23 cubs over the 32 year period in which she was studied. Bear No. 56 probably survived for so long because she was in a remote area away from roads and was very shy. A wild bear that reaches 25 years of age would be considered old, as most bears don't survive nearly that long.

OLDEST OF THE OLD

European brown bear Andreas was born around 1963, captured as a cub and then trained to stand up and shuffle his feet like he was dancing. For the next 30 years he was taken from town to town with a painful chain through his nose to dance for tourists. One of Greece's last dancing bears, he was rescued in 1993. When he arrived at the Arcturos Bear Sanctuary Andreas was already old and blind, but in the large forested enclosure he shared with other rescued bears, he lived for another twenty years. When Andreas died on May 24, 2013, he was approximately 50 years old, the oldest bear known.

ONE BEAR
YUPI THE MEXICAN POLAR BEAR

Yupi was lying on the concrete floor of her enclosure, legs splayed out in spread-eagle fashion, trying to stay cool in the stifling heat. The sun beat down and there was no shade. She was panting.

When Yupi saw people at the underwater viewing window, she plunged into the water and swam up to them. The people smiled and laughed. In a few minutes, they left. Yupi watched them through the window. When they were gone, she swam back to the edge of the pool, hauled herself up on the concrete and resumed lying in the same position she was in just a few minutes before. The evaporation of water from her fur cooled her down a bit and provided temporary relief from the heat.

Yupi was born blind and helpless in the wilds of Alaska, the most northerly state in the United States. Her world was an earth or snow **maternity den** that her mother had dug months before. It was a tiny sanctuary, insulated from the cold, dark winter nights. It was made up of a narrow entrance tunnel and two chambers.

In the spring, sometime between February and April, Yupi's mother broke open the den entrance. By that time, Yupi's eyes were open. She had grown to a weight of 10 – 15 kilograms (22 – 22 lbs.). Her mother left the den and soon Yupi and her brother did too. For a week, they didn't go far, but Yupi's mother was hungry. When she thought her cubs were strong enough, she set off to find food. The cubs followed.

They were traveling to the edge of the sea ice, where Yupi's mother could hunt seals. Yupi still relied on her mother's milk for nourishment, as well as her protection from potentially dangerous adult male polar bears. Whenever Yupi felt threatened, she ran to her mother to be comforted. For the next two and a half years, until Yupi was **weaned**, she would follow her mother and learn how to survive and prosper in the foreboding Alaska environment.

But Yupi never got that chance. Details are sketchy but it's known that in March 1992, near the village of Wainwright on Alaska's north shore, Yupi's mother was shot by a hunter who didn't know she had cubs. Yupi and her brother became orphans.

If they had remained on their own in the wild, they might have starved or been killed by an adult male polar bear. But on March 18, United States Fish and Wildlife officials caught them and took them to the Alaska Zoo in Anchorage. Although there is conflicting information about how old Yupi and her brother were when they arrived at the zoo, it's thought they were somewhere between 3 months and 2 years of age.

The zoo was just a waystation until a placement elsewhere could be found for the cubs. Another zoo in the historic City of Morelia, Mexico, approximately 300 km (186 miles) west of Mexico City, wanted a polar bear. That's where Yupi was sent.

On May 31 Yupi was shipped in a small crate by Alaska Air to San Francisco, California and then to Guadalajara, Mexico before being taken to the zoo in Morelia. If her mother hadn't been killed, she would still be with her on the ice. But now Yupi was experiencing strange new sounds, vibrations, odours and sights that she could not understand.

Mexico is far to the south, a very different place in every way from Alaska. The climate is very warm. While average temperatures in Morelia are 14–25 °C (57–77 °F), it can go up to 38 °C (100 °F) in the summer. In Alaska, the average temperatures are minus 30- 11 °C (minus 22-52 °F). Only rarely does it go as high as 18 °C (64 °F). Mexico is also far more humid.

Polar bears have dense fur, a layer of blubber, snowshoe-sized feet and many other adaptations that make them superbly adapted for cold weather. They are not made for living in the heat of Mexico.

Since polar bears evolved to live in the cold, it's not surprising they may have difficulty coping in warm climates but, even so, they are often able to survive for decades in poor conditions.

When Yupi arrived at the Morelia Zoo, she was placed in an old grizzly bear enclosure. Her living space was small, mostly concrete, much of it painted white, the colour of snow and sea ice. She didn't have much shade and her pool water was not cooled or refrigerated. She also had no air conditioned area where she could retreat from the heat, even during the hottest parts of the summer.

Yupi could walk around her small enclosure but there was nothing much else to do, so she spent a great deal of her time just sitting or lying on the concrete. When her keepers went home for the day, she was confined in a small, barren concrete room until the next morning when the keepers returned to work. Each day was the same.

Yupi was surrounded by walls. A fence would have been better because she could at least have seen some of the world beyond the barriers that enclosed her. She would have been stimulated by more odours and sounds, too, which were blocked out by the solid walls.

I first visited Yupi in 2005 with my Zoocheck colleague, Julie Woodyer. From the underwater viewing window, we could see her lying on the concrete at the edge of her pool. As soon as she saw us, she leaped into the water and made her way to the window. She seemed curious and wanting something interesting to do.

Mexico is not an appropriate place for polar bears. Even if improvements were made to Yupi's conditions, she would still be better off if she were moved to a larger, more natural space, especially in a more polar-bear-friendly climate.

Yupi didn't know it then, but that first visit was the start of a long campaign by Zoocheck to try to help her and other polar bears in Mexico. The campaign started small with a report about Yupi and then communications to the zoo itself. That was followed by Zoocheck's staff and polar bear experts going to the zoo to assess Yupi's conditions and to meet with zoo staff. Sadly, those meetings with the zoo managers didn't go anywhere. Local animal welfare groups began to speak up and even organized protests occurred at the zoo.

As Yupi's plight became big news, local and national politicians started to speak out, too. The zoo felt pressured into making some changes. They added overhead shade cloth, a sand pit, sprinklers and an air conditioner to her night area. Later they reopened an old visitor viewing station. But still Yupi remained at the zoo.

In 2015 the Governor of the State of Michoacan got involved and helped arrange for another expert Zoocheck team to visit Yupi to conduct a health and welfare assessment. The team found that Yupi was in poor shape. Her teeth were especially bad. Some teeth were rotten and others broken and painful. Her gums were infected. The Zoocheck team corrected all of Yupi's dental problems and sent a report to the Governor and the zoo.

After a lot of negotiation an agreement to move Yupi to a large, natural enclosure at the Yorkshire Wildlife Park in the United Kingdom was signed. A shipping crate was sent to the zoo and Yupi was trained to enter it. All of the plans for Yupi's transport were moving along well until the zoo and the Governor suddenly pulled out of the agreement with just a couple of weeks to go. It was a massive shock and stopped the plans to get Yupi out of Mexico.

While I was finishing this book, Zoocheck was working on new strategies to get Yupi to a better home in the United States. Her prospects were looking good. Yupi was close to feeling real grass beneath her feet, being able to make herself a day bed, experiencing new sights and smells, meeting other polar bears and playing in the snow, but that didn't happen. On November 12, 2018, Yupi suddenly passed away. She never did see a new home, but at least her years of boredom and suffering had ended.

5

BEAR CAPTIVITY

BARREN CAGES

Toronto's old Riverdale Zoo opened in the late 19th century. It's now closed. I visited the zoo as a kid and I remember seeing bears living in barren, concrete enclosures behind thick, steel bars. I've visited hundreds of zoos since that time and many of them still keep bears in those kinds of cages.

It wasn't until the early 20th century that there was any real change in the way bears in captivity were housed. It occurred when German animal dealer-zoo operator Carl Hagenbeck began using moats to contain animals in zoo exhibits. His idea soon spread around the world. Since then, bears have usually been kept in what are called grotto or island exhibits. A grotto is an enclosure surrounded by walls at the sides and back with a moat at the front, while an island exhibit is an area of land primarily enclosed by a moat. The moats can be dry or filled with water and are designed so the animals can't climb out. Unfortunately, most enclosures are small, barren and unnatural. I've seen them in zoos throughout the world, including in the United States and Canada.

BEAR WELFARE

Animal welfare is very important, especially to intelligent animals like bears. For a bear to achieve good welfare they must be physically and psychologically healthy and must be able to engage in natural, species-typical movements and behaviours that use the adaptations they've developed to survive. If they can't, then their welfare probably isn't very good.

In captivity, behaviour-based husbandry can help bears achieve good welfare. It means understanding bears and then creating environments that satisfy their needs. It allows them to do the things they behaviourally or genetically expect to do, such as foraging, making day beds, denning or hibernating, to name just a few.

The Five Freedoms of Animal Welfare

Checking the principles described in The Five Freedoms is a good first step toward determining if a bear's welfare is acceptable or not. All five should be satisfied.

1. Freedom from thirst, hunger and malnutrition (appropriate food and fresh water)

2. Freedom from discomfort (appropriate shelter and comfortable climate)

3. Freedom from pain, injury and disease (humane treatment and veterinary care)

4. Freedom to express normal behaviour (large natural spaces and rich, complex environments)

5. Freedom from fear and distress (places to hide and to feel safe and secure)

ROOM TO EXPLORE

In zoos around the world bears are usually not provided with very much space to roam and explore. It seems like the exhibit designers didn't really consider how wide-ranging, intelligent and active bears are.

According to renowned zoo architect David Hancocks, big animals need big spaces. Certainly bears are big animals that live in very large spaces in the wild. The home range of American black bears can be tens or hundreds of square kilometers, while polar bear home ranges can be up to 96,525 square miles (250,000 km²) in size. Most bear exhibits are thousands or millions of times smaller than the spaces wild bears inhabit.

All bears are carnivores but the amount of meat in their diet varies from species to species. Polar bears consume the highest percentage of meat. Giant pandas consume the lowest. Some bears, like the sloth bear, prefer a diet of insects. Sun bears eat a lot of fruit. The other species enjoy a mix of plants and animals, taking advantage of seasonal abundance.

How much space does a captive bear require? A good starting point would be at least one acre of natural, forested enclosure for every two adult bears. That's still not very much space but for many captive bears, it would be a big improvement.

While captive bears can't be provided with as much space as wild bears, most facilities that keep bears should do better. If they can't, perhaps they should reconsider keeping bears at all.

BEARS NEED THINGS TO DO

Wild bears are active, traveling, hunting or foraging for food and doing all of the other things that bears do. American black bears may forage for insects, berries and other food for up to 18 hours a day. Sun bears search for fruit in the trees and build elevated day beds to rest, while Giant pandas spend a considerable portion of each day moving from one cluster of bamboo to another, munching on the shoots and stems. In captivity natural activities are reduced or even eliminated, leaving bears with very little to do. That can lead to frustration, boredom and abnormal behaviours, such as pacing or sleeping all the time.

Bears that live in large, natural enclosures with real earth, trees, bushes, pools and other natural features seem to do much better. So even poor bear enclosures should be made better by adding furniture and things like branch piles, large logs, rotting stumps, leaf litter, sandboxes, climbing structures, elevated platforms, wooden ladders, walkways, hammocks, segments of fire hose, cardboard boxes, beer kegs, and ice blocks, to name just a few. There are many more possibilities. Adding items to an enclosure is a component of **environmental enrichment**. It's good to do, but the goal should be to provide bears with large, natural enclosures that are already complex and interesting. If an enclosure needs a lot of added enrichment, it's probably too small and boring for the bears.

GOOD NEWS FOR BEARS

Ricki's Rescue: Ricki was a familiar sight at Jim Mack's Ice Cream in Pennsylvania. She paced back and forth, alone, across the concrete floor of her tiny cage. There was nothing else for her to do. After 16 years, Ricki was rescued. A lawsuit filed by four Pennsylvania residents and the Animal Legal Defense Fund led to an agreement that saw Ricki released to the Wild Animal Sanctuary in Colorado. She now enjoys a 15-acre enclosure with her friends Coco, Josie and Jesse.

MY FEET FEEL GOOD

All bears evolved to live on the natural ground surfaces they encounter in the wild. They are comfortable standing and walking on those surfaces which also offer them different smells, tastes and textures, as well as opportunities for activity, such as digging, turning over rocks and logs or foraging for ants and other insects. Bears are not adapted to live on hard surfaces like concrete or **hardpan** (hard,

compacted earth) like you see in many zoo exhibits. Hard floors can cause damage to the skeletal system, as well as muscle strain, foot lesions, footpad cracks, sores and other health problems.

Concrete floors can also absorb heat during the day, causing discomfort or even thermal burns to bear feet, and the heat may be released by the concrete at night, resulting in almost constant discomfort to the bears that live on it.

A COMFY BED

Many wild bears construct comfy day beds on the ground or, for some bears, in nests in the trees. It's their quiet place to rest, relax and just get away from it all. Some bears also dig earth or snow dens seasonally for hibernation and they give birth in them. But many bears in captivity don't have private spots to get away from the rigours of zoo life and that can be stressful. Bears kept with other bears may also need to get away from each other. Not being able to can result in aggression, stress and suffering.

MEALTIME DELIGHT

Bears naturally spend a lot of time foraging for food. Giant pandas and Sloth bears have specialized diets, but most bears eat a wide variety of foods. For example, American black bears may eat grasses, nuts, berries, snails, insects, crayfish, frogs, small mammals, bird's eggs and a lot more.

Finding food is a key activity for bears, but in captivity they usually have their food given to them. Bears need to forage so creating ways for bears in captivity to search for food can help keep them physically and psychologically healthy. Scattering food around the enclosure, hiding it in hollow logs, placing food in hard to reach locations, and painting jam or honey on furnishings or walls are just a few of the ways that foraging opportunities can be created for captive bears. It is called **food enrichment**.

ZOO ILLUSIONS

Many zoos have big, flashy, expensive exhibits that are supposed to mimic the wild and make people feel they're in a natural setting with bears or other animals. They're called **landscape immersion** habitats, but they are more like fake movie sets than the real wild. Many are filled with fake rocks or rock structures made with a spray-on concrete called **gunite**, artificial logs and trees or simulated tundra. The big new expensive, landscape immersion exhibits may look good to visitors, but they may not be very good for the animals.

WEIRD BEHAVIOURS

Rocking, head bobbing, repetitive pacing or swimming back and forth or in circles, paw sucking, tongue playing, and other abnormal behaviours are common in captive bears. These repetitive behaviours are called stereotypies and they only occur in captivity. A bear who displays them is probably frustrated and bored. They are the bear's way of trying to cope, but they don't work. It's the environment that causes the unnatural behaviours, so unless that changes, the bears will continue to display them.

GOOD NEWS FOR BEARS

Happier times for Circus Bears: Molly performed for many years as a dancing bear in the circus, where she was called Clyde, before being sold to a private menagerie. During her years of confinement and abuse Molly developed terrible stereotypic behaviours, rocking back and forth and bobbing her head repeatedly. She was rescued and brought to Canada to the Bear With Us sanctuary on December 9, 1994. She was provided with a densely forested enclosure approximately 3,717 m² (40,000 ft²) in size and, soon, a friend, a bear named Yogi, came from another circus. Yogi's owner had heard Molly's story and wanted to give her a companion. Molly lived to be 30 and Yogi is still alive.

TWO BEARS
WINNIE, THE WORLD'S FAMOUS BEAR

While waiting at the White River train station in Ontario, Harry Colebourn glanced out the window and was astounded to see a man with a young bear on the platform. Since Harry was a veterinarian with a keen interest in all animals he had to get off the train to have a look.

Harry was originally from England but had moved to Canada when he was 18 years old. He worked a variety of jobs until he enrolled at the Ontario Veterinary College in 1908. He graduated as a veterinary surgeon in 1911. That summer he accepted an offer to work for Canada's Department of Agriculture in Winnipeg.

Soon Harry joined the 18th Mounted Rifles as an officer before being transferred in 1912 to the Thirty-fourth Fort Garry Horse. Since Harry was already a trained officer when World War I broke out in August 1914, he volunteered for duty. On August 23 he boarded a train going to a military training camp in Valcartier, Quebec. He would officially be part of the Canadian Army Veterinary Corps (CAVC). At the time, large numbers of horses were being used in the war, so CAVC veterinarians like Harry were needed to provide care and to tend to wounded animals at the front.

When Harry approached the little bear on the train platform, she immediately tried to play with him and even climbed up onto his lap. The man said she was for sale. Apparently, a trapper had shot the cub's mother, not knowing she had babies. Only one of them survived. The trapper didn't want the responsibility of caring for a growing bear cub, who was probably about six months old at the time.

The train whistle blew, alerting everyone that the train would be leaving very soon. Harry had to make a decision. He asked how much the man wanted for the bear. He replied twenty dollars. So Harry gave him the money, picked up the cub and they both boarded the train.

When his superior officer asked Harry what he was doing, Harry replied that he would take care of the cub and that she could stay at camp with him. He also said he had already named the cub Winnipeg, after his company's home town. During the long rail journey to Quebec, the cub's name was shortened to Winnie.

At camp, Winnie followed Harry everywhere and the two would play games together. When Harry had duties that required him to temporarily leave the camp, the other soldiers pitched in, playing with Winnie and walking her. But each night Winnie slept under Harry's cot with Harry snoozing above.

A month later Harry learned that his company was being sent to England. More soldiers and horses were needed for the war effort. Harry told his superior officers that Winnie should go too. On October 3 they both boarded the S.S. Manitou and set sail for England.

The ship landed in England on October 17. At the Second Canadian Infantry Brigade Headquarters, Winnie became the CAVC's mascot and a pet to many of the soldiers.

Soon Harry received orders to remove Winnie from camp. He was being sent to active battlefields in France and Winnie could not accompany him. Harry didn't have too many options for where Winnie could be cared for. But the London Zoo had just opened a new bear exhibit called the Mappin Terraces and Harry decided to place her there until the war was over.

On December 9, 1914, Harry and Winnie set off for the zoo. During the ride, Winnie sat on Harry's lap. They were met at the zoo entrance by a keeper who took them to the Mappin Terraces. Winnie's collar and leash were removed and she was introduced to a couple of brown bear cubs. Harry thought everything looked good, so he said goodbye to Winnie, promising that after the war they would return home to Winnipeg together.

Winnie and the brown bear cubs got along well and became friends. A larger bear in the enclosure was a bit more surly, but soon he and Winnie were getting along too. The keepers said Winnie was the calmest, most gentle bear they had ever seen, and they would sometimes take people in to meet her. On occasion, children would even ride on her back.

While many stories suggest that Winnie's time at the zoo was enjoyable, I don't think it was. If the Mappin Terraces were to be built today, it would be called outdated and inappropriate. They were small grotto enclosures made mostly of concrete, with almost nothing natural in them. The bears they contained, including Winnie, must have been bored and frustrated, because they were unable to do anything that bears want to do.

World War I lasted for four years. During that time Harry visited Winnie as much as he could and thought she was doing well. When the war ended in 1919 and Harry was getting ready to go back to Canada, he decided Winnie would be happier at the London Zoo so he left her there.

When Winnie was about eleven years old, a young boy named Christopher Robin visited the zoo. He fed Winnie and gave her a hug. His father, renowned author A.A. Milne, stood nearby watching. That evening Christopher told his father that his teddy bear Edward had changed his name to Winnie-the-Pooh, so instead of telling bedtime stories about Edward, they became stories about Winnie-the-Pooh. The Pooh part of Winnie's name came from a swan Christopher used to have as a pet. Eventually the stories became a book entitled *Winnie-the-Pooh* which was published in 1926. *The House at Pooh Corner* followed in 1928. The books made Winnie famous around the world and people flocked to the zoo to see her.

On May 12, 1934 at the age of 20, Winnie passed away. I hope that people today realize that Winnie's life wasn't very good at all. *Winnie the Pooh* is a wonderful story, but Winnie's real story is not a happy one. Her mother was killed and she was captured. Then she was sold to Harry Colebourn, who it seems was devoted to Winnie and only wanted the best for her, but at the London Zoo she spent the remainder of her life in a barren exhibit. The life Winnie led is not the kind of life any bear should live.

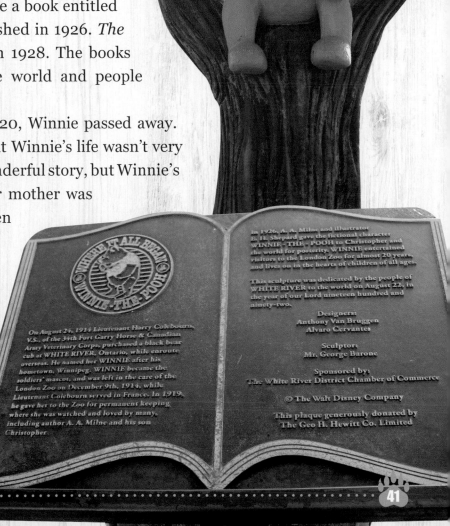

USING BEARS

BEARS ON DISPLAY

Hundreds or possibly even thousands of bears were kept captive in Ancient Rome. They were used in the Roman games, public entertainment events in which animals were hunted or forced to fight each other, next to human gladiator battles, chariot races and other activities. Ancient Egyptian pharoah Sahure, the second ruler of the 5th Dynasty, imported Syrian brown bears and kept them on leashes. Bears were also kept in the menagerie of ancient Egyptian King Ptolemy II. One of the more unusual captive bears was a polar bear kept at the Tower of London in England in the 13th century. The bear was brought out every day and chained by the River Thames. Since that time, bears have been a staple in zoos and wild animal collections around the world. Almost every traditional zoo has had a bear.

RENT A PANDA

Two Giant pandas arrived at the Toronto Zoo on March 25, 2013 as part of a rental agreement with China. The pandas would be at the zoo for five years before being sent to the Calgary Zoo for an additional five years. The Toronto Zoo was required to pay the Chinese government $1 million a year to rent the pandas. The zoo claimed getting pandas was for conservation, but many people question that idea. They say it's more about the zoo trying to make money than saving pandas and that it diverts attention away from the challenges faced by pandas in the wild.

JAPAN'S BEAR PARKS

The first of Japan's eight bear parks opened in Noboribetsu on the northern island of Hokkaido in 1958. The parks were developed to provide facilities where orphaned and unwanted Asiatic black bears and brown bears, which are native to Japan, could be placed. However, since bears are popular animals and people wanted to see them, the parks became tourist attractions and breeding was encouraged. Today visitors watch circus-type shows and are allowed to feed the bears or get their photo taken holding a bear cub. Through the years, bear numbers in the parks grew until hundreds of bears were housed in barren, overcrowded, concrete-floored enclosures. They suffered from lack of space, inactivity, unsanitary conditions, injuries from fighting, and other health issues. People have expressed concern for years, but improvements have been slow. The creation of Bear Mountain in 2010 by Kamori Kanko, the company that owns Noboribetsu Bear Park, might be the first real sign of change. Hopefully this 15-hectare, naturalistic enclosure housing 13 bears will encourage other facilities in Japan to change to a more humane way of keeping bears.

DANCING ISN'T FUN FOR BEARS

In India, Asia and parts of eastern Europe dancing bears have been a common sight for hundreds, or even thousands, of years. Often cruelly and painfully restrained with chains or ropes attached to rings in their noses, the bears were walked around during the day so tourists could pay to watch them dance or, in modern times, to have their photos taken with them. At night they were tethered to the ground or tied to fences, trees or rocks. Most of these bears were illegally taken from the wild as cubs and then beaten into submission so they could be used on the street. India made dancing bears illegal in 1972, but the practice continued for many years. Other countries have also established laws prohibiting dancing bears. Thankfully the laws have resulted in a big decrease in dancing bear numbers and in some areas an end to this abusive practice.

GOOD NEWS FOR BEARS

No More Dancing in the Street: In 2002, the Indian wildlife protection organization, Wildlife SOS, began rescuing dancing bears. On December 18, 2009, they rescued Raju, the last dancing bear in India. More than 600 bears were rescued in total, and placed in three separate sanctuaries. Europe's last three dancing bears were rescued on June 15, 2007 by the Four Paws Foundation. Misho, Svetla and Mila were relocated to a 30-acre sanctuary south of the City of Sofia, Bulgaria. After living their lives on chains, the three bears were finally free.

BEAR BAITING

Bear baiting, where bears fight dogs, was banned in England when the Cruelty to Animals Act was passed in 1835, but the practice continues today in remote regions of Pakistan. A brown or Asiatic black bear is secured to a post by a 2 - 5m (6.5 - 16ft) rope or chain around its neck or one leg, then trained fighting dogs are set loose. Sometimes

a bear's canine teeth have been removed and the claws dulled so the bear doesn't have too much of an advantage over the dogs. It's a nasty activity that can result in severe injuries or death to both the bear and the dogs. A number of groups have been trying to stop bear baiting and it does seem to have been reduced. With any luck, it will soon be gone.

BEAR FARMING

An estimated 7,000 – 10,000 bears live on bear farms in China, with an additional 2,400 bears on farms in Vietnam and approximately 1,350 in Korea. Most farmed bears are Asiatic black bears, but Brown bears and Sun bears are also farmed. They are kept so their bile can be extracted — through a tube painfully inserted through their abdomen into their gallbladder — for use in Traditional Medicine (TM). The bears are kept in cages, called crush cages, that are so small the bears can't stand up or turn around. The bears are often underfed, dehydrated, injured, diseased and psychologically damaged. Numerous synthetic bile alternatives are available, so there is no need to cruelly confine bears on farms.

THREE BEARS
THE UNCAGING OF JASPER

Jasper probably had distant fragmented memories of life in the forest with his mother, when she looked after him, teaching him the skills he'd need to survive as an Asiatic black bear in the wild. He may have remembered following her through the forest, rooting for grubs, insects, mushrooms, fallen fruit, nuts and other food items, and cuddling up beside his mother at night, feeling warm and safe from snakes and wild boar they had encountered. One day that all changed.

The details are sketchy but Jasper was captured, probably after his mother was also captured or perhaps even killed. He was put in a cage and transported a long distance. He was scared and crying. It was the first time in his life he had been alone, he had no idea what was happening, and he didn't know where his mother was. He wanted to be next to her.

Eventually, Jasper's cage was moved into a strange concrete-

floored room. He could see brick walls, a metal roof, unusual objects and other caged bears, just like him.

Jasper's cage was small and he couldn't stand up properly. The cage, raised up off the ground, had metal bars on all sides and even on the floor, so Jasper had to stand on them instead of the soft natural surfaces of the forest floor. His feet hurt. He wanted to run away but couldn't. He could just stand on all fours, sit or lie down.

Every day a man came and gave Jasper food and water. When the man left, he turned off the light. Eventually the man inserted a large metal tube into Jasper's stomach and lowered part of the cage roof, so Jasper had to lie down on his stomach. A fluid dripped from inside of him, through the tube and into a pan on the floor below. He was in something called a "crush" cage and the liquid dripping from the tube was his bile. He didn't know that a young woman named Jill Robinson had started trying to help bears just like him.

The first time Jill visited a bear farm, she was taken into a dim room. It was hard to see, but she could hear bears making deep "popping" sounds. As her eyes adjusted, a scene was revealed that she would remember for the rest of her life. A number of tiny metal cages, raised up off the floor, each imprisoned a bear. Two bears had missing paws. Others had broken teeth, from biting the bars. Their bodies were riddled with scars. The skin around a hollow metal tube inserted into one bear's belly was red and infected. She knew this tube was how the "bear farmer" extracted its bile.

When Jill felt something touch her arm, she turned. A bear had reached through the bars of its tiny prison. Jill took the bear's paw in her hand. It broke her heart when the bear gently squeezed her fingers,

After she left, Jill couldn't stop thinking about the bears, so she decided to publicize their plight. In time, her efforts began to pay off.

In 1995, the local government closed the bear farm and gave the bears to Jill and her team to rehabilitate. Three years later, Jill founded the Animals Asia Foundation to help China's estimated 7,000 – 10,000 bile bears. In 2000, Animals Asia and the Sichuan Forestry Department signed an agreement to rescue 500 bears and to work together to end bear farming.

A proper sanctuary was needed to house the bears, so Jill and her team established the China Bear Rescue Center near the City of Chengdu. The sanctuary would provide rescued bears with space to roam, grass to walk on, earth to dig in, structures to climb, water to swim in and safe comfortable places to sleep.

While all this was going on, Jasper just lay in his crush cage, pulling and gnawing on the bars, each day the same as the one before — until one morning Jasper's small cage was taken from the room and put onto the back of a truck. It was placed next to other cages and for the first time Jasper could clearly see the faces of other bears.

The truck made its long journey on bumpy roads. Jill and her Animals Asia team met the truck when it arrived at the sanctuary. There were many bears to examine, 63 in total that day, but the workers had to be careful. When approached, the bears made popping sounds and growled. Their fear was understandable. For all those years, the only people they had seen were the bear "farmers," who had caused them pain and suffering.

Jasper had been in the cage so long it had rusted shut. He was given a sedative to make him sleep, so he wouldn't be too alarmed

when the cage was cut open and veterinarians examined him. He was like a skeleton with fur. His muscles had wasted away from years of disuse. The many years of rubbing against the metal cage had caused a great deal of fur loss and his teeth were badly damaged from biting the bars. Like the other bears that came with him, his mind was probably damaged too. The vet tended to his injuries and other medical issues.

When Jasper awoke, he was in a larger cage. He had space to stand up, turn around and stretch. It was more room than he had experienced in many years. He also had soft straw to sleep on.

Jasper grew stronger with each passing day. He was given access to an indoor bear house –a den– so he could practice walking. Eventually he went outside. He must have been amazed when he first felt the softness of grass beneath his feet, and when he looked toward the sky and saw no bars.

As Jasper's health slowly improved, he became more active, curious and playful. He splashed in the pool, ran, climbed, manipulated objects and wrestled with other bears. He also took on the role of comforting other bears when it seemed they were not feeling safe or secure, and he became friends with new bears that came to the sanctuary.

Jasper was fortunate to be rescued, but there are thousands of other bears just like him that still need help. Jill Robinson and the Animals Asia Foundation continue to rescue bears and work to end bear bile farming in China and in other countries where it takes place.

In 2017, the Vietnam government invited Animals Asia to come and end bear bile farming there. The very last caged bears will be rescued by 2022. That might seem like a long time from when the decision was made, but setting up places for the bears to live, raising the funds required to keep them happy and healthy for the rest of their lives, assessing their health and welfare and then transporting them is a massive task that takes careful planning and time to organize.

HUMANS AND WILD BEARS

HUNTING BEARS

Since prehistoric times bears have been hunted for their pelts, meat, trophies, sport or because they were feared. Today bear hunting for fun and recreation is widespread. It can include baiting bears with food to attract them to where hunters wait, tracking them with dogs, using snares or just searching them out and making a kill. The most commonly hunted bears in North America are black bears, but brown bears and polar bears are also hunted as well. During the 19th and early 20th centuries, many North American populations of black bears were severely reduced by hunting.

MORE THAN A MOUNT

Trophy hunting of bears occurs in many parts of the world. In North America, many hunters pay big money to kill a grizzly or polar bear, so they can mount their head or even their entire body as a display back home. They claim they're helping generate jobs for local people where

the bears are found and contributing to conservation. But a 2014 study by the Center for Responsible Travel says wild bear tourism (bear watching) generates more money than shooting them dead.

GOOD NEWS FOR BEARS

Buy a Hunting License, Save a Bear: An innovative strategy was used by the Raincoast Conservation Foundation (RCF) to protect British Columbia's bears and wolves from trophy hunters. Since hunting licenses are required for each region in which trophy hunting takes place, the RCF purchased an exclusive 24,700 km² (10,579 square miles) hunting license for $1.3 million. This move effectively ended trophy hunting in that entire area of British Columbia and today there are more bears and wolves then ever. In August 2017, the efforts of the RCF, other groups and thousands of citizens paid off even more when the Government of British Columbia announced it was ending the sport hunting of grizzly bears in the province for good.

Bear watching tours that allow members of the public to see bears in the wild are growing in popularity around the world

BEAR TOURISM

Tourists visiting North America pay thousands of dollars to observe wild brown bears in British Columbia and Alaska, or grizzly bears in Alberta. It's clear that live bears are worth more than dead bears, so hopefully bear-hunting tours everywhere will soon be replaced by bear-viewing tours. It makes sense. A tourist viewing a bear one day allows another tourist the next day to see that same bear. If the bear is shot dead by a hunter, that bear is gone for good.

GOLDEN GALLBLADDERS

The trade in bear body parts is one of the biggest threats to wild bears, especially in regions of Asia, because the gallbladder of a bear is so valuable. The gallbladder is a small organ where a fluid called bile, produced by the liver, is stored before it is released into the small intestine. A single bear gallbladder can get thousands of dollars in the Asian Traditional Medicine market. Poachers may also seek other bear parts, including fur and paws. In Korea, a bowl of bear paw soup can cost as much as $1,000. In May 2015, a bear carcass was found without paws or gallbladder near Sechelt, British Columbia. Thirty-four states in the United States have banned the trade in gallbladders, while Canadian provinces Quebec and British Columbia have banned the possession and trade of bear gallbladders and paws. The rest of the states and provinces should do the same.

FOUR BEARS
WOJTEK THE SOLDIER BEAR

The young Iranian boy had a bag and something inside it was moving. It was 1942, during World War II. Polish soldiers encountered the boy during a rest stop on their way to the City of Tehran. One of them opened the bag and found a tiny Syrian brown bear cub, the size of a teddy bear, looking back at him. The soldier lifted the cub out of the bag and cradled him in his arms. The soldier and his comrades instantly fell in love.

The bear's mother had probably been killed by a hunter, so he could be taken and sold for use as a dancing bear. A civilian **refugee** named Irena Bokiewicz, who was part of the military convoy, loved the cub as well. She wanted to buy him but didn't have any money, so she convinced Lieutenant Anatol Tarnowiecki to purchase the cub. He asked the boy if he owned the bear and he nodded. Anatol knew the boy needed food, so he gave him food, a penknife and some money in

exchange for the bear. The soldiers then made their way to a Polish refugee camp near Tehran.

Irena looked after the cub for several months and then he was donated to the 2nd Transport Company, later called the 22nd Artillery Supply Company, Polish II Corps. In short order, the soldiers decided he needed a good Polish name, so they came up with Wojtek, which is usually spelled Voytek in English. It means "he who enjoys war" or "smiling warrior."

As the soldiers' mascot, Wojtek was fed condensed milk, fruit, and whatever else could be spared. When the soldiers had to travel to Iraq and then through Syria to Palestine, Wojtek went with them.

When they arrived at the camp in Palestine, the Commanding Officer (CO) ordered the soldiers and Wojtek to report to him right away. Remarkably, once he saw the little bear, he agreed to let Wojtek stay. But he also said he must be enrolled as a new recruit in the Polish army. His enlistment would ensure he could travel with the Corps.

Wojtek settled in to camp life and slept in bed with one of the soldiers, at least when he was small. Over time he became bolder and started to explore and cause mischief. On more than a few occasions,

Wojtek broke into the cookhouse and ate whatever food he could find. He also learned how to use the showers and often depleted the water supply, much to the chagrin of soldiers who wanted to get clean.

The soldiers often wrestled with Wojtek, even when he weighed several hundred pounds. He loved to play and was always careful not to hurt anyone.

The camp had another resident wild animal, a monkey named Kaska, given to the soldiers by the director of a zoo they had visited. Kaska didn't like Wojtek. When she first encountered him, she threw stones at him from a rooftop. She continued throwing things at Wojtek everytime she saw him. Poor Wojtek just lay down and put his paws over his eyes, probably hoping that Kaska would go away. Even when they were kept on different sides of the camp, Kaska often found Wojtek and threw things at him, then escaped on the back of a large dog who also lived in the camp.

But Wojtek did find another animal friend. A Dalmatian dog belonging to a British soldier became Wojtek's best friend. At one point Wojtek left camp and headed into the desert, possibly to find water. The Dalmatian's barking alerted everyone that Wojtek had left. The soldiers found Wojtek way out in the desert and brought him back to camp in the cab of a truck.

Wojtek was sometimes rewarded for good behaviour with beer. It became his favourite drink. He also developed a fondness for cigarettes. He didn't smoke them, however. He ate them and actually preferred them when they were lit.

When the transport soldiers were ordered to drive to Iraq to pick up barrels of oil, they followed orders and took Wojtek along. The British soldiers in the new camp loved Wojtek and, just like before, he got into lots of mischief. He also performed a great service once, when he went to the showerhouse to have a shower and found a spy hiding inside. The spy was so terrified of Wojtek that he gave himself up, and Wojtek was credited with preventing an attack.

As World War II progressed, the soldiers' duties changed from transporting oil and supplies to transporting soldiers from various locations to Alexandria in Egypt. From there they would then be sent to Italy to help the British and American troops that were already there. The transport soldiers — and Wojtek — left for Italy on February 13, 1944. Soon they would be transporting guns, shells, mortars and other weapons of war to the front, where the fighting was.

Wojtek's first trip to the front was scary. Each time a bomb exploded, he tried to jump

into the lap of the driver. When they reached their destination, a line formed to transport heavy ammunition from the truck to the storage area. Wojtek stood watching and then took up a position in the line as well, and helped pass the shells along. He became known as the bear that carried artillery shells.

It wasn't long before the German forces were pushed back, opening the way for the Polish and Allied troops to move onward to the City of Rome. When they arrived, they donated Kaska the monkey to the zoo so she could have monkey companions. But things didn't work out and soon she was back with the soldiers. A little while later, she had a baby and her quarrels with Wojtek ended.

World War II went on and the transport soldiers continued to drive heavy ammunition to the front, and Wojtek was with them, until the German leader Hitler was killed and the war was over. The soldiers celebrated and so did Wojtek.

It took a year until the Polish soldiers were shipped out to Scotland and then another year before they could return home. But that wasn't possible for Wojtek. He could never go back to the wilds of Iran, so a decision was made for him to go to the Edinburgh Zoo.

Soldiers that had befriended and cared for Wojtek said their good-byes, knowing they would probably never see him again. But during his years at the zoo, some of the former

Polish soldiers came to visit Wojtek, occasionally throwing him a lit cigarette and talking to him in Polish.

Wojtek had lived a very unusual life, unlike any other bear, ever. And even though it was not the way a bear should live, there is little doubt that it was always interesting, exciting and changing. No doubt Wojtek had times when he was happy and other times, such as when bombs were exploding at the front, when his life might not have seemed very good at all. But confinement in the zoo, spending his remaining years in a relatively barren concrete island exhibit, must have been hard. Every day — the conditions, the scenery, the routine — was the same as the day before.

Wojtek died in December 1963. Numerous memorials commem-orating his life have been erected, including plaques in war museums in London, United Kingdom and Ottawa, Canada. On May 18, 2013, a statue of Wojtek was unveiled in Park Jordana in Krakow, Poland. On November 7, 2015, in Edinburgh's Princess Street Gardens, a bronze statue was unveiled — of Wojtek and a Polish army soldier walking in peace.

The Greater Yellowstone Ecosystem is the largest intact area of wild country in the United States. Large tracts of wilderness are essential to the survival of bears, wolves, bison and other large wild animals.

11

GETTING ALONG WITH BEARS

SHARING WILD SPACES

Bears are generally wide-ranging animals. Their home ranges are determined largely by food availability, **social hierarchy** (the presence of other dominant bears) and, for females, breeding and denning needs. If food is plentiful, the range of a bear can be relatively small, like a Sun bear in a dense tropical forest full of fruit trees. But if an area isn't food rich, a bear's range might have to be bigger. That can be a problem in areas where expanding human populations mean less space available. Good bear habitat may be fragmented by roads, cottages and other rural development, or bears may be disturbed by human activity and driven away. If we want to ensure that bears have a secure future in the wild, we need to protect large, undisturbed areas of good bear habitat, do everything we can to stop bears being killed, and make every effort to prevent human-bear conflict in regions where people and bears share the landscape.

GOOD NEWS FOR BEARS

Back to the Wild: An underweight grizzly bear cub was found near Cranbrook, British Columbia in June 2014. His mother had been killed by a hunter. He weighed just 48 lbs (22 kg) and was given the name Littlefoot. He was sent to the Northern Lights Wildlife Society and nursed back to health before being released back into the wild in August. He had attained a healthy weight of 143 lbs (65 kg), giving him a very good chance of survival. Littlefoot was tagged and fitted with a satellite collar that would allow him to be tracked for 18 months. The Northern Lights Wildlife Society has rescued and released eleven other grizzly bears and most of them have done well.

In June 2015, a black bear cub named Cinder was released to the wild after spending nearly a year recovering from severe burns to all four of her paws. She received the burns during a major wildfire in the Methow Valley of Washington and was starving when she was found. Her rescue was prompted after a rancher saw her crawling along the ground on her elbows and knees. She was sent to the Idaho Black Bear Rehabilitation facility where her feet healed and she gained 90 lbs (40.8 kg) in weight. Cinder was released near where she was found in an area with lots of food.

COEXISTING WITH BEARS

Human-bear conflict situations can result when hungry bears cause property damage to homes, buildings, cars, beehives or other human valuables. Conflicts can also result when people are afraid and believe that bears automatically pose a threat to their safety, even when they don't. That belief often results in bears being needlessly shot when they are near people.

Preventing problems before they happen is the best way to help bears. Residents living in bear country should make sure they don't attract bears. Managing potential food sources, such as garbage containers, pet food containers, barbecures, beehives, bird feeders and fruit trees is a must. Towns and cities should ensure that industrial garbage containers, collection depots and garbage dumps are managed so they don't attract bears or allow them access to it.

There are many programs to educate the public about coexisting with bears and preventing human-bear conflict. One of them is run by the Get Bear Smart Society in British Columbia, Canada.

BEAR ATTACKS

A lot of people are extremely afraid of bears, but that fear is often based on myths and misunderstandings. To some extent, bears have a bad reputation because whenever a bear attack occurs, it's big news, featured in media all over the world. Most people don't realize that bear attacks are rare; they don't know about the thousands of encounters between humans and bears that occur every year that don't result in any problems at all. Walking by myself in the wild, I have encountered numerous bears and they have all just gone on their way once they've seen that I pose no threat to them.

Of course, it would be incorrect to say that bears are completely harmless or that they pose no risk at all because bear attacks do happen. There have been human fatalities due to polar, brown and black bears and even sloth bears in India. According to one study, in North America from 1900 until 2009, there were 59 incidents involving American black bears which resulted in 63 people being fatally mauled. Every one of those incidents was tragic, but considering the hundreds of thousands or millions of human/black bear interactions, it is a very small number. The chance of being killed by a black bear is less than that of being killed in a car accident, or by bees, or from being struck by lightening. It's good to take precautions in bear country, but a fear of bears shouldn't stop anyone from enjoying the wild. It's just important to be bear-smart about it.

ENCOUNTERING A BEAR

Keep calm. Most bears are as surprised as you are and given some time will just retreat.

❶ <u>Don't run</u>. Bears can move very quickly and running might prompt them to chase you. Stand still and if you are in a group, stand together.

❷ <u>Give the bear space</u>. Back away slowly and speak to the bear in a soft voice. Don't move toward a bear and avoid looking a bear right in the eye.

❸ <u>Wait</u>. If you are unable to move away from a bear, wait and allow the bear to go on its way.

❹ <u>Don't panic</u>. Bears are smart and often very curious. Sometimes they'll stand up on their hind legs to look at you or to try to pick up your scent. They may be frightened and huff and make popping sounds. These signs are usually not signs of aggression.

❺ <u>Don't attract bears to your campsite</u>. Bears are attracted by food, so when camping in bear country make sure your food is stored a suitable distance away from where you sleep, preferably on a rope suspended in a tree. Doing that is safer for both you and the bear.

BEAR REHABILITATION

Black bear cubs have been successfully rehabilitated and released back into the wild in North America for many decades. In Russia, the International Fund for Animal Welfare's Bear Rescue Center has returned more than 200 bear cubs to the wild. Different rehabilitation strategies have been used, including introducing orphaned cubs to **lactating** mother bears with cubs of their own, or raising cubs in captivity and then reintroducing them to the wild when they are sufficiently old and large enough to be able to fend for themselves Other important factors include finding a suitable release site with abundant natural food sources. Hundreds of bears have been sent back to live in the wild by bear rehabilitators.

FIVE BEARS
A NEW HOME FOR VINCE

In January 2000, during a cold Wisconsin winter, Vince was born. He was a tiny American black bear weighing between 280–450 g (0.62–0.99 lb). He was just 20.5 cm (8.1 in) from nose to tail and covered in grayish, down-like hair. He nestled up against his mother, enjoying her warmth and attention. Vince's eyes were shut and would remain that way for another 4 – 6 weeks. He'd start walking, a little bit, when he reached 5 weeks of age. Vince relied on his mother's milk for nourishment for about 30 weeks, and reached a weight of 18 to 27 kg (40 to 60 lb) in just 6 months time.

At 1 ½ - 2 years, a bear like Vince would be fairly independent and soon after set out on his own. But that didn't happen for Vince, because he and his mother were not free.

It's legal for private citizens in Wisconsin to keep and breed black bears, and that's what Vince's owner did for more than 20 years.

Vince's parents lived in a 4.5 x 4.5 meter (15 ft X 15 ft) chain link enclosure with a concrete floor. They could walk only a few paces in any direction before encountering the fence.

Vince's mother was bred every year. That would not occur in the wild because females don't breed until their cubs have left to live on their own, usually at around 2 years of age. In November a bale of straw was placed in her concrete block den and the door was locked. She was imprisoned inside and forced to hibernate. In the wild, hibernating bears may wake up several times during the winter and even, on occasion, leave the den. Vince's mother didn't have that opportunity.

In February, when the owner could hear crying, he lured Vince's mother out of the den and shut the door, separating her from her baby. Then he removed Vince and his siblings. The bond between mother bears and their cubs is incredibly strong, so forcibly separating them that way, especially when the cubs are so young, is horribly traumatic to both of them. And Vince's mother was forced to go through that every year, just so her cubs could be sold to someone for a profit, possibly even someone without a state license to keep bears.

In Wisconsin where Vince was born, the Department of Natural Resources requires owners of captive bears to complete and submit a form each year. But the information people provide is on an honor basis and isn't always verified. So, if a female bear has three cubs and a breeder wants to sell one to an individual without a license, it's easy to report only two cubs, leave the third cub unreported, and sell it. Reportedly, only about 10% of captive wildlife owners even bother to complete this form.

Vince could have faced a depressing life stuck in a small cage, shuffling a few paces in one direction and then another, but he was lucky enough to be aquired by reformed hunter and new bear advocate, Jeff Traska.

After giving up hunting, Jeff embarked on his own personal study of black bears. He thought his research would be well served by obtaining a bear, one rescued from life in a small cage. He promised himself that satisfying the bear's needs would be his highest priority. He had observed bears in small cages and in the wild, so he knew that bears in small cages were unable to tap into any of their own natural abilities or do anything that bears normally do.

Jeff decided to create an environment in which Vince could use his natural abilities, engage in natural behaviours, and

thereby thrive. He thought that building something that was good for Vince would also create an amazing educational opportunity for anyone who came to see him. When Jeff spoke about his plans to other bear owners, some told him they wanted to increase the size of their cages too, but officials said it wasn't allowed. Jeff carefully reviewed the regulations and found that a bear enclosure didn't have to be the minimum size required by the state; it could be much larger.

Jeff constructed a pen more than double the 4.5 x 4.5 meters (15 x 15 ft) regulation size. It was 12 x 12 meters (40 x 40 ft). The enclosure was given approval from the Department of Natural Resources and Vince arrived in March of 2000.

Jeff bottle-fed Vince and introduced him to a more natural world by enhancing and expanding Vince's enclosure. With Jeff's encouragement, Vince explored his living area, began climbing trees, foraging for food, hunting insects and swimming in the pond — utilizing more of his natural instincts and abilities than he'd had the opportunity to do before.

Wisconsin
**BLACK
BEAR**
Education
Center

A Place to Learn

During Department of Natural Resources (DNR) inspections, officials became interested in updating Wisconsin's approx-imately 40 year old set of rules and regulations for captive animals. They wanted to use Vince's enclosure as a model for discussion. Vince's "open top" enclosure design and photos were presented at a DNR-hosted meeting of captive wildlife owners. Sadly, some of the other captive animal owners didn't see larger, open top enclosures as a great development; they saw it as a way to lose money. If they were required to build better cages and provide more bear-friendly conditions, it would reduce the profit they made from selling the animals.

Jeff fought for more space and better conditions for bears for four years. His modest goal of requiring just 111 square meters (1,200 square feet) of space per bear was not reached. The rules were amended to require a tiny 37 square meters (400 square feet) per bear, and just 18.5 square meters (200 square feet) for each additional animal. For a wide-ranging, active, intelligent animal, that's a remarkably tiny space in which to live. It's just 6 meters by 6 meters (20 ft x 20 ft), smaller than most city backyards.

Jeff also contacted his state representative repeatedly for six years urging that all captive wildlife facilities be inspected semi-annually, but they said they didn't have money for inspections. He then asked them to come inspect his facility. He was surprised when someone showed up during the hibernation period! They didn't see a bear, but completed their checklist, approved Jeff's facility once again, and then left.

Vince has grown to be a healthy, seemingly well adjusted bear. He forages for food, such as ground wasps, ant larvae and natural sedges and grasses. As new and expanded sources of enrichment are provided, his intelligence, curiosity and playfulness become more evident and lead to a better understanding of his needs.

After Vince's arrival, Jeff rescued two other bears, Sunny and Moon, from a breeding operation. Most recently they were joined by Red Sky, an orphaned cub.

Through the years, Jeff kept expanding his facility and it is now one of the best in the United States, with more than 10 acres of natural, bear-friendly space for the four residents. His facility shows just what can be done if you keep the needs of the bears in mind.

During Vince's remarkable journey, Jeff Traska established the Wisconsin Black Bear Education Center, a sanctuary focused on creating understanding and awareness about black bears. He has plans to conduct bear rehabilitation by assisting orphaned and injured bear cubs and preparing them for release back into the wild.

Vince has experienced a life unlike the life he would have had in the wild. But it is better than the life of many other bears in Wisconsin and elsewhere, including his own mother. Hopefully, Vince's legacy

HOPE FOR BEARS

Bears are loved throughout the world, but they are facing some very tough times. Six of the eight bear species are now threatened with extinction. Habitat fragmentation and destruction is a threat to bears in many areas of the world, especially in Asia. Polar bears face unique challenges as their northern environment is being altered due to climate change. Legal hunting and illegal poaching cause the destruction of tens of thousands of bears every year, while live adult bears and cubs are still removed from the wild for a variety of purposes. And human-bear conflict has led to many bears needlessly being destroyed.

Bears in captivity face their own set of challenges. The thousands of bears like Jasper who are held on bile farms endure bleak, awful lives and their plight must be addressed. Vince's counterparts who are kept as pets and bears that continue to be used in entertainment need attention, too. So do the many thousands still confined in zoos where they suffer from lack of space and exercise, under-stimulation, overcrowding, injury, disease and psychological problems.

It may seem bleak and overwhelming, but there is reason for hope. Things are starting to change for the better. Traveling shows with bear acts are disappearing and street dancing bears will soon be nothing but a memory. Areas of bear habitat have been protected and more will be in the future. With each passing year, ever increasing numbers of people around the world are speaking up for bears and actively working to help them. I've had the pleasure of meeting many of them.

Jeff Traska's interest in bears led him to start the Wisconsin Black Bear Education Center, a facility that shows a kinder, behaviour-based way to address the needs of bears in captivity. Jill Robinson's experience and passion resulted in the formation of the Animals Asia Foundation with a goal to end bear farming. The efforts of Jill and her amazing team of people have freed hundreds of bears from their cages of despair. There are many more people just like them and every year I meet new dedicated advocates working tirelessly to help bears in the wild and in captivity.

I am particularly pleased to see new sanctuaries being developed and large, natural enclosures now being recognized as better for bears. I'll never forget my visits to the Bannerghatta Bear Rescue Center in India, the Wisconsin Black Bear Education Center and numerous other facilities with large, natural bear enclosures. After seeing so many listless bears in zoo exhibits around the world, it is refreshing to see bears foraging, digging dens, running, playing, climbing tall trees, making day beds and disappearing into the vegetation. In recent years, natural bear enclosures have become more common. The Romanian Bear Sanctuary, Colorado's Wild Animal Sanctuary and the Bornean Sun Bear Conservation Center all provide large, natural enclosures for bears. Large bear enclosures have also been constructed in sanctuaries in Hungary, Greece, India, Canada, the United States and elsewhere.

Even some zoos have moved in that direction. In The Netherlands, the Bear Forest in Ouwehands Zoo is a 2 hectare (4.94 acre) semi-natural habitat enclosure that provides a home to rescued former

circus or dancing bears. A few other zoos also
have large bear enclosures, such as the 6.4 acre
polar bear facility at Norway's Skandinavisk
Dyrepark (Scandinavian Wildlife Park) and
the Alaska Wildlife Conservation Center.

The large, natural bear enclosures are a better, more humane way
of housing bears in captivity. Today there should be zero tolerance of
small, barren bear cages and enclosures.

Many good things have happened for bears, but much more must
be done to prevent their suffering and to secure their future in the
wild. I sincerely hope that the information in 5 Bears and the stories
of the bears I've profiled will motivate you to help bears, wherever
they may be. I believe the world would be a much poorer place if
bears were no longer out there in the forests, valleys, mountains,
deserts and tundra. We don't want a world where the only bears we
have left are some sad survivors in a zoo. I hope you agree.

WAYS TO HELP BEARS

1 Learn about bears and the challenges they face both in the wild and in captivity. Check the internet and your local library for information about bear issues.

2 Inform your family, friends, classmates and neighbours about how bears are treated in captivity (such as in zoos and bear farms) and how they are threatened in the wild (from habitat loss, trophy hunting and other causes).

3 Start a project to educate your school about the plight of bears around the world or organize a fundraiser for a bear protection project or bear sanctuary.

4 Do not attend circuses, shows or performances that feature wild animal acts.

5 If you encounter bears in poor zoo conditions, make an official complaint to the zoo, your local humane society and the appropriate government agency. Ask your parents to help you draft your complaint.

6 If your town or city destroys nuisance bears, urge them to develop a program to prevent human-bear conflict and to encourage peaceful, coexistence with bears.

7 If your province or state does not support bear cub rehabilitation and release, urge them to adopt policies or laws that allow it. Orphaned cubs should be given a chance to live a natural life.

8 Speak out against bear hunting for sport or trophies.

9 Support laws that protect wild bears and the habitats they need to survive.

10 Support legitimate sanctuaries that provide large, natural pens for bears rescued from cruel conditions.

ORGANIZATIONS THAT PROTECT BEARS

Animals Asia
www.animalsasia.org

Arcturos
www.arcturos.gr/en

Bear With Us Sanctuary and Rehabilitation Centre
bearwithus.org

Black Bear Rescue Manitoba
manitobabearrehabilitation
centre.ca

Four Paws
www.four-paws.org.uk

Free the Bears
freethebears.org

Get Bear Smart Society
www.bearsmart.com

Great Bear Foundation
greatbear.org

Raincoast Conservation Foundation
https://www.raincoast.org

The Wild Animal Sanctuary
https://www.wildanimal
sanctuary.org

Wildlife SOS
wildlifesos.org

Wisconsin Black Bear Education Center
wisconsinblackbears.com

World Animal Protection
www.worldanimalprotection.ca

Zoocheck
www.zoocheck.com

GLOSSARY

Behaviour-based husbandry: A method of animal housing, care and management based on the behaviour of animals.

Bile: A dark fluid produced by the liver that assists digestion in the small intestine.

Carnivorous: A meat-eating animal.

Carrion: The decaying flesh of a dead animal.

Environmental enrichment: Providing furnishings, objects, foods, sights, smells, and sounds, and making changes in management strategies to keep animals physically and psychologically stimulated.

Food enrichment: Providing different kinds of foods in different ways.

Gallbladder: A small organ that stores bile from the liver.

Gene: A genetic unit that is transferred from a parent to offspring that often contains coding for a characteristic of the offspring.

Grolar bear: The offspring that result from the mating of a grizzly bear and a polar bear.

Grotto: A concrete exhibit with walls on the sides and back and a moat at the front.

Gunite: A mixture cement, sand, and water mix sprayed through a pressure hose to produce a concrete-like layer on a surface.

Hardpan: A natural earth surface that has been packed down into a concrete-like consistency.

Hyperphagia: A condition of excessive hunger and increased eating.

Insectivorous: An animal that feeds primarily on insects and small invertebrates.

Island exhibit: An exhibit that is mostly or entirely surrounded by a wet or dry moat.

Keystone species: A species that plays a key role in the functioning of the ecosystem it lives in.

Lactating: The process of a mother animal producing milk for her baby.

Landscape immersion: A design concept in which visitors are in, or seem to be in, the natural habitat of the animals.

Maternity den: An earth or snow den in which a mother gives birth.

Metabolic rate: The rate of processes in the body that allow an animal to survive.

Non-retractable: Unable to be drawn back in.

Omnivorous: An animal that eats both animal and plant materials.

Pappilae: A small rounded, bump on the skin or body.

Pigeon-toed: Walking with the toes pointing inward.

Pizzly bear: The offspring that result from the mating of a polar bear and a grizzly bear.

Plantigrade locomotion: Walking flat footed with the toes and metatarsal bones on the ground.

Refugee: A person who has been forced to leave their home due to natural disaster, war or human rights violations.

Social hierarchy: The ranking of animals in a group, often the result of fighting or dominance displays.

Scent receptor: Part of the sense of smell containing cells that detect odours.

Stereotypic behaviour: Meaningless, repetitive movements, common in animals in captivity but not found in wild animals.

Weaned: A mammal is weaned when it is no longer in need of its mother's milk.

INDEX

Bibliography

Appleby, M.A., Winnie the Bear, *The True Story Behind A.A. Milne's Famous Bear*, Dominion Street Publishing, Winnipeg, MB, Canada, 2011

Bieder, Robert, *Bear,* Reaktion Books, London, UK, 2004

Brown, Gary, *The Bear Almanac, A Comprehensive Guide to the Bears of the World*, Lyons & Burford, Publishers, New York, USA, 2013

Dolson, Sylvia, *Bear-ology, Fascinating Bear Facts, Tales & Trivia*, Pixyjack Press, Masonville, CO, USA, 2009

Fair, Jeff & Lynn Rogers, *The Great American Bear*, Northword Press, Minocqua, Wisconsin, USA, 1994

Lindburg, Donald & Karen Barogona, *Giant Pandas: Biology and Conservation*, University of California Press, Berkeley, CA, USA, 2004

Mulvaney, Kieran, *The Great White Bear, A Natural and Unnatural History of the Polar Bear*, Houghton Mifflin Harcourt, Boston, MA, USA, 2011

Orr, Aileen, *Wojtek The Bear, Polish War Hero*, Birlinn Ltd., Edinburgh, Scotland, 2010

Poulsen, Else, *Barle's Story, One Polar Bear's Amazing Recovery from Life as a Circus Act*, Greystone Books, Vancouver, BC, Canada, 2014

Raffan, James, *Ice Walker, A Polar Bear's Journey Through the Fragile Arctic*, Simon and Schuster, Toronto, ON, Canada, 2020

Read, Nicholas & Ian McAllister, *The Salmon Bears, Giants of the Great Bear Rainforest*, Orca Book Publishers, Victoria, BC, Canada, 2010

Russell, Charlie & Maureen Enns, *Grizzly Heart, Living Without Fear Among the Brown Bears of Kamchatka*, Vintage Canada, Toronto, ON, Canada, 2002

Shushkewich, Val, *The Real Winnie, A One-Of-A-Kind Bear*, Natural Heritage Books, Toronto, ON, Canada, 2003

Stirling, Ian, Polar Bears, *The Natural History of a Threatened Species*, Fitzhenry & Whiteside, Markham, ON, Canada, 2011

Tak, Bibi Dumon, *Soldier Bear*, Wm. B. Eerdmans Publishing, Grand Rapids, Michigan, USA, 2008

Thomas, Keltie, *Bear Rescue, Changing the Future for Endangered Wildlife*, Firefly Books, Richmond Hill, ON, Canada, 2006

Watkins, Victor, *Bear Sanctuary*, Bear Sanctuary Publications, UK, 2011

PHOTO CREDITS